Cystitis
A Hidden Message

Cystitis
A Hidden Message
By Diana Silvia Nicolaci

Illustrated by Ruby Concetta

Copyright © Diana Silvia Nicolaci

All rights reserved. No part of this book may be reproduced by any mechanical, photographic, recording or electronic process without prior permission from the author.

The information contained in this book is intended as a guide only. The author is not a medical practitioner and advises that you seek medical advice before following any of the practices in this book.

All the information in this book was gained through personal experience, and knowledge obtained through the practice of meditation and the study of other books and philosophies.

ISBN: 978-0-646-55562-1

Dedication

I would like to dedicate this book to all the women who suffer with chronic recurring cystitis.

It is my hope and my intention that your suffering ends and that you live your life in freedom with full health and joy.

Introduction

This book was written for women who suffer with recurring cystitis (urinary track infections). I wrote this book after a 20 year struggle and vowed if I ever found a cure I would write a book to help others.

I believe if I had this book at the beginning of my journey I would not have had to suffer for 20 years with cystitis, although maybe I wouldn't have been open to the ideas in this book at that time.

Cystitis

A *Hidden* Message

I have found that cystitis has revealed a hidden message to me and I believe women who suffer with chronic recurring cystitis have the same message to hear.

I suffered with recurring cystitis for a period of 20 years and I now believe I have the authority to speak about it to others. It is my intention to help others to overcome this horrible dis-ease and begin to heal.

Any recurring illness carries with it a hidden agenda. If we are willing to dig deep we will be rewarded and begin to understand ourselves and who we truly are. The hidden agenda is a mystery that we will now set out to unravel.

Cystitis is another word for urine infection. When you have an infection you probably dread going to the toilet and yet you will have to go constantly, feeling pain and burning with each drop.

Chills run through your body and night calls from your groin are a constant reminder of the unease that you feel.

Rocking in front of a heater in the early hours of the morning and needing a hot bath, leaves you feeling lost and alone. There is a feeling of people looking through you and wanting to hide, but where do you go?

You take endless antibiotics until you become allergic to them. When this happens you feel a dread and hopelessness, where do you turn when antibiotics no longer work? Who do you turn to when doctors can no longer help? Where do you go when you have tried alternative therapies only to have the urine infections return?

Is there a way out?

The way out is to go within.

To go within is the way out and it took me 20 years to learn this wonderful secret of truth.

This book is designed to take you through an emotional and spiritual journey. I believe by doing this you will unblock *hidden* parts of yourself that must come to the surface so that you can live in freedom and move forward in your life. This process does not take a day or a week, it may take you years as it did me, but it is worth every effort. What I am saying is that the process of change is an ongoing one. You can and will feel better as soon as you put into practice the things that I suggest in this book, but change is an ongoing journey and an exciting one.

My intention in writing this book is not to give you false hopes but to help you understand the emotional and spiritual blockages that lock you into the pattern of recurring cystitis.

Millions of women and some men suffer with cystitis, (urinary tract infection) some times resulting in kidney infection and thrush.

If you have had reccurring cystitis then you already know all of the suggested remedies, i.e. drink plenty of water, don't over indulge in alcohol, wipe from front to back, limit your caffeine intake, wear cotton undies, drink cranberry juice and so on and so on.

Once you have tried all of this and you still keep getting cystitis then what do you do? Where do you go?

Searching For Answers through Doctors

Doctors are wonderful and we need them in our quest for health. It is important to make sure that you have had all the necessary medical tests to rule out any underlying cause for your infections.

The first sign of cystitis is having to go to the toilet more frequently. Then as the day or night goes on you will begin to feel pain and burning when you pass urine. The colour of your urine may look more cloudy and perhaps smell strong. Sometimes you can literally see blood in the urine. You may also have a fever along with the pain. The best thing to do at this stage is to drink lots of water, you can add 1/3 of a teaspoon of bicarbonate of soda to help ease the burning and hopefully flush away the infection, you could also try some citravescent powders such as Ural available from the chemist.

Often trying to flush the infection away does not work and you could be in for an awful night of pain and chills. It is my suggestion that you see a doctor as soon as possible for antibiotics. If not treated the infection could reach the kidneys.

The tests listed here are what I personally experienced. Some specialists may suggest other tests or procedures.

****

Doctors will normally ask you how long you have had the symptoms for and ask you to give them a urine specimen which they will check to see if there is any blood in the urine. They will send it off to be tested to see if it is an ascending infection (caused by bacteria) or a descending infection (descending down from the kidneys). They will then prescribe antibiotics.

****

When you come in again and again for the same problem you may be sent to see a Urologist who may send you for an X-Ray examination of the urethra, known as urethrography. A radiopaque fluid is inserted into the bladder through the urethra, while passing this fluid X-Rays are taken to see if there is any narrowing or if there are any other abnormalities.

****

A Urologist may suggest that you have your bladder stretched (blown up) because you are going to the toilet too frequently. Telling you that your bladder is too small after a consultation of about 5 or 10 minutes!!!!!!

After talking to other women I came to realize that this is a procedure done regularly and sometimes over and over on the same patient.

****

Another procedure is to have a dilation of the urethra, an operation in which the urethra is widened and scraped for removal of polyps or for taking specimens of tumours or other growths.

****

It may be suggested to have a colonoscopy which is an examination of the entire colon and rectum, to rule out any trouble with the bowels.

****

Often a low dose of antibiotics is prescribed over a 3 month period, but some women still have an infection whilst taking them. Another form of treatment is to prescribe Septrin Forte, taking 2 immediately when noticing an infection.

****

An ultrasound of the kidneys could be done to rule out trouble in this area.

Your doctor could even suggest you have a curette in which the cervix is cauterized. This is done with a heated instrument (known as a cautery) it destroys tissue and is used for the removal of warts or other growths. It is performed after abortion or for removal of small tumours and for obtaining a sample of the endometrium for examination to diagnose any gynaecological disorders.

****

After taking so many antibiotics you can become allergic to them and are then left with limited choices of antibiotics. I became allergic to Penicillin, Septrin Forte and Macrodantin.

I was told my urethra was a bit too exposed and this may be the problem. One doctor suggested that if I was having oral sex this may be causing it. Another doctor told me that women weren't created well. I was told that maybe I wasn't having as many attacks as I thought and

was probably just having back pain, or not drinking enough water.

Women tend to think that there is something physically *wrong* with them when often this is not the case.

After going through test after test more often than not nothing shows up.

There is also far too much emphasis on hygiene being the cause of cystitis. E-coli bacteria shows up in the urine and therefore thought to transfer through sexual activity, not wiping the right way (front to back) when going to the toilet, tampon strings, nylon underwear etc. In my opinion you can become overly obsessed with hygiene even becoming anxious going to the toilet.

If your doctor starts guessing and making statements that make you feel uneasy and you have been through as many tests as you can tolerate then it is time in my opinion to look elsewhere for answers.

Searching for Answers through Natural Remedies

Seeing a Naturopath

Naturopaths seem to point to Candida (a yeast infection) as being the cause of cystitis. I believe the over use of antibiotics kill the useful as well as the harmful bacteria and upsets the body's balance therefore triggering a vicious cycle.

Candida which is a fungal infection is treated with a strict diet avoiding all food that contains yeast, sugar and starch for a period of at least five weeks to three months.

Foods to avoid are mushrooms, yeast supplements, vegemite, marmite, yogurt, cheese, buttermilk, sour cream, pickles, vinegar, tomato products, soy products, tofu, wine, beer, preserved meats, peanuts, canned fruit, dried fruit, grapes, melon, white flour, white rice, white spaghetti, ice cream, and soft drinks, anything containing sugar.

The fungi (Candida) normally inhabit the intestines and vagina and when these areas are not healthy symptoms of infection occur. Fungi can also multiply in alkaline conditions, especially where there is warmth and a plentiful supply of sugars. Semen is alkaline, whereas the vaginal mucous membranes are slightly acidic so this may also be contributing to the problem. Washing the area after sex with warm water can help.

Cystitis sufferers are prone to vaginal thrush and antibiotics will usually worsen the problem. You can see the dilemma that women face.

A high fibre diet with plenty of vegetables and whole grain foods is suggested. Vitamin C in powder form and Lactobacillus acidophilus and Bifida bacteria are a form of naturopathic treatment.

Seeing a Homeopath

Homeopaths use a system of therapy which uses minute doses of medicines that produce the symptoms of the disease treated. It is a system of medicine developed by German physician and chemist, Dr Samuel Hahnemann (1755-1843) based on the principle of "like cures like". It is reported that his work was prompted by his observations when working of himself with various drugs. When he took large amounts of quinine, for example, this brought on the symptoms of malaria, when he took tiny amounts of quinine the symptoms disappeared. Subsequently he developed the theory and practice of homoeopathy based on the principle that what a substance can cause it can also cure. The case of snake bite victims and anti venom may come to mind when understanding this theory.

Homeopathy views many symptoms to treat the underlying causes for ill health. In this context, mental and emotional symptoms are taken into account. Questions may be asked about diet, sleep, lifestyle, and about some mental and emotional aspects to the illness.

Homeopathic medicines are derived from plant, animal, mineral and micro biological sources. The medicines can be given as liquid or globules. Occasionally there is a temporary worsening of the symptoms prior to improvement.

Seeing a Naturopath or a Homeopath is up to you and can help if you are ready to heal but if you are still finding that you are not getting the answers you need, then keep reading.

After searching and searching and running around in circles, I felt afraid and alone and thought I would never find a cure.

But I did find a cure and I am now free of cystitis but more importantly I am free to live my life happier and unafraid. It has taken me a long time to come to this point and I am hoping that through this book I can help other sufferers to be set free. I hope that by reading this book you will not have to go through the struggle alone and wait as long as I did.

Health comes from within. Although diet is an important part in overcoming cystitis, diet alone will not make a difference. You must look at yourself as a whole person and therefore you need a whole treatment plan for yourself.

If you have searched for answers everywhere and have now found yourself reading this book, I believe this is the perfect book for you.

The Answers Are Within

I have come to understand that the way you think and feel about all aspects of your life holds the key to health and happiness.

How do you *feel* about cystitis? What do you *think* about cystitis? If you haven't had a bout of cystitis for a while do you think, I haven't had it for a while I must be going to have an attack soon? When you go to the toilet if you feel the slightest uncomfortable feeling when urinating do you think, "I must be getting it again"?

I believe women who have recurring cystitis begin to fear it, they dread it, and they wait in expectation of its return. You must begin to understand that what you **resist persists** and what you **fear** you **attract** to you.

I would like to ask you to look at cystitis in a different way. As you look at it in a different way you will begin to unravel the mystery of why you have had this particular problem for so long. Instead of working against it, work with it.

Begin to look at cystitis as a friend or acquaintance. When and if it returns think of it as though you have just bumped into an old friend. Start to think that this friend has bumped into you to leave you a message. You may not fully understand the message but you are beginning to. Be thankful that this friend has taken the time to leave you this message. You don't have to fear this friend, you don't have to dread bumping into this friend, just know that you are beginning to understand the message that this friend has come to tell you. Know that you are beginning to have less and less in common and that you will soon be saying farewell.

Now if cystitis is a friend your whole perception must change. It is not your enemy and there is nothing to be afraid of. You may dread its return or feel uncomfortable when you have its company but if you want desperately to be rid of recurring cystitis attacks you have to stop, turn around and take notice. You cannot run away from this friend or hide.

Your body is your closest friend. It will tell you over and over again that something is wrong until you have to stop and listen. What is it trying to tell you?

To pass urine is the last point of releasing fluid. Is your body trying to tell you that you are becoming stagnant? Are you holding onto emotions or ideas that are no longer in your best interest? Do you need to become more fluid in your ways? Perhaps you aren't even aware of being stuck or stagnant, but your body at the deepest level is aware of it and is trying to tell you. You may think your life is just fine the way it is, but your body and your spirit knows there is a better way of life waiting for you, if only you will take the time to listen and this is the way it has chosen to get your attention.

I would like to give you an example of what I believe you must do for yourself. If you have a bucket of dirty stagnant water and you want clean fresh water, you have a couple of options, you can tip out the dirty water and put in fresh water (a quick fix), or you can gradually and continually pour clean water into the bucket of stagnant water until there is only clean fresh water remaining.

Both options work just as effectively. But remember the quick fix of emptying the bucket and putting in fresh water will only work for a time. If you *leave* the bucket with fresh water, after time it will again become stagnant and dirty. If you gradually and *continually* pour fresh water into a bucket you will have clean fresh water all of the time.

Health is not a tablet, although antibiotics work and are necessary, they are a quick fix. You cannot experience lasting change over night but just as we can end up with fresh water in a bucket through gradually pouring in clean water, you can become healthy through gradually pouring in health and letting go of what is no longer needed.

How do you pour in health? What does this mean?

A good way to pour in health is to begin writing positive things about your self. I believe writing is very powerful and suggest you do this. Buy yourself a lovely note book or journal to write in. You can choose to keep your notes or to burn or shred them after you have finished with them it's up to you. I kept mine for a time but eventually burnt them when I felt the time was right. You can choose to keep them a day a week or a year, or however long you need them, it's up to you. But I ask you to write daily. Give yourself half an hour a day to write, and don't say you don't have the time, because this is part of the problem. You *must* make time. You can get up earlier in the morning and have some alone time, or you can do it in you lunch hour, or before bed. Just set aside half an hour each day for this.

Example of Words that are helpful

I am willing to let go of the need for cystitis.

Health surrounds me and permeates me.

I am comfortable with my sexuality.

I am completely at ease with myself.

I love and accept myself.

I can cope with change.

I let go of the past with love.

I am only influenced by love.

I always support myself and I am progressing.

I am doing the best I can.

☺

I always take care of myself.

I let go of other people's opinions.

Love surrounds me and permeates me.

I live in the moment of now.

I am doing the best that I can in this day.

I let go of the need to be pissed off.

I let go of the need to blame others.

Whatever you think of me is none of my business.

I have a wonderful relationship with my partner.

I know I am worthy of being completely healthy.

I am ready to allow healthy thoughts to flow.

Let your writing flow and make up your own words and sayings that feel right for you.

    Write one page of positive things and say them out loud and take notice of how you feel. Do you feel that they are true? Take notice of what is going on inside your mind. How do you feel? What are you thinking? Just take notice.

    Now write down how you feel, pour out all your feelings and again take notice of any negative thinking pattern. Begin to understand what is going on in your mind.

    Choose an easy affirmation one that makes you feel good and continue saying it to yourself over and over for the day. Say it as often as you can remember during the day quietly in your mind.

    Continue this process on a daily basis. After doing this for a couple of week's notice how you feel. Do you feel happier? Do you feel lighter? Are you noticing changes in yourself?

Whenever you are afraid that cystitis will return, try to go deeper and find out what you are really afraid of. In my opinion it is extremely important in times of fear to say to your self over and over the following statements.

I am surrounded by love. Love flows to me and through me at all times.

I am surrounded by health. Health flows to me and through me at all times.

When you have a bladder infection, take this time to pamper yourself. Think of this as a sacred time. Your friend has come to you once again and you need to be alone so that you can begin to understand why this friend has returned. Never beat yourself up and get angry because it has come back to you. Take some quality time for yourself.

Have a hot bath and *relax* in it. Burn some essential oils specific in the help of cystitis (listed at the end of this book). Listen to some soft music. As you lay in the bath say your positive affirmations over and over.

Say to yourself although this has returned I am getting better each day. My body is beginning to heal in each moment.

Use this time to ponder your feelings and to write. Through writing you will begin to notice a link to your having an attack of cystitis and a particular emotion you have. For instance I noticed a link to my cystitis and the emotion of sadness.

Sadness is one word but has many aspects, betrayal, anger, shame, regret, guilt, failure, control, blame, not trusting.

When you have an attack of cystitis write down what you were thinking prior to your attack, (the days leading up to it). Were you feeling sadness? Where you feeling angry or anxious? Write down how you were feeling and keep a diary so you can see if there is any pattern in your thinking that needs to be challenged.

Do you feel pressured by your partner to have sex when you really feel uncomfortable with it? Can you talk

☺

about it with your partner or are you afraid too? Do you give in to sex just to keep your partner happy and resent him for it? Do you feel dirty after sex or guilty? Do you think God will judge you for the way in which you engage in sex? Or are you just uncomfortable with who you are in general? Asking these questions will help you understand what's going on inside you.

Music can also be a wonderful instrument in healing, if you listen to the right music that is in tune with you. Some songs can help release emotions buried within. You will instinctively know what music feels right for you. It may be a song that makes you cry. That's ok cry but afterwards make sure you put something uplifting on.

While you are going through your cystitis episode it's good to spend time pondering but there is a time for everything. Dwelling on negativity brings in more negativity, don't deny your feelings but don't dwell on them either. The main point is to identify what you are feeling and then let the feeling go. Say to yourself I am safe with whatever life brings to me, and try to refocus.

Bring some laughter into your day. Phone a friend that makes you feel happy or watch a funny movie.

Understand that as you begin pouring in healthy and positive thoughts, negative thoughts will start to surface. Just as with the bucket of stagnant water, while clean water is pouring in, dirty water is surfacing and pouring out.

Write down a list of any negative thoughts that come to your mind and write down any negative comments that were said to you when you were younger about sexuality. You may think why am I talking about sexuality? Isn't this about my bladder problem? The bladder is connected to the energy centre of the body associated with sexuality. I will go into this in more detail later in this book.

What thoughts were instilled into you by your mother, father, siblings, friends, religion etc regarding sex? Can you remember any saying that was repeated often while you were growing up that wasn't very positive? My mothers favourite saying was "sex is dirt and all men want is dirt", not a very positive slant on love making!!!!!

After doing this exercise you might feel like crying or you might even feel angry. It's good to be able to understand that these feelings are still buried within you and that it is these feelings that have helped you to stagnate.

Keep writing down your positive thoughts and say them to yourself over and over. Allow your self to be joyful, realise that life isn't all about being serious, it's also about having fun and enjoying happy times. Put photos around your house of happy times, not just photos that you look good in, but photos where you are really having fun, even if you don't look that great in the photo remember how you felt when it was taken.

Life isn't about how good you or your loved ones look or how perfect you are. It's about living, it's about laughing and crying, it's about feeling ugly and getting over it.

Go slowly through this book. If you truly want to heal then you will, but you need to be willing to do the work. The work is exciting, interesting, it's about you, digging deep and understanding who you are. Isn't that worth the effort?

☺

Words

Words are my companion in times of distress
Words are a gift beyond measure
Words can astound and lift the spirit
Words are a part of who I am
Words will flow in times of need
Even in times of great confusion, my words are given
There are times of unknowing
Yet words can comfort surprisingly
they can comfort and lift up the spirit
because words are a connection.
They connect thought with spirit
they connect one with the other
they connect man with women
women with child
friend with foe.

*Words when given at the appropriate time are a treasure beyond amounting.
Words are a gift just one more of the many gifts of life
How thankful all must be to have so many gifts*

☺

Now let us continue

If you have had a childhood experience that you remember as a bad experience but you feel that it really hasn't affected you as an adult, I suggest you think again.

Try this exercise and see how you feel afterwards. Hold your pen in your left hand if you are right handed and in your right hand if you are left handed. Recall the experience as best as you can and write it down. When writing it down in the opposite hand to the one you are used to writing with, it slows you down and in doing so will bring you back to the time of the experience. It will also be in child like writing and this all helps in the process of bringing the feelings to the surface. These feelings may have been buried deep inside you because as a child you couldn't express yourself or more than likely there was no one who you could express yourself to, or had the time to listen to you. But now you are the adult and the one who can listen. You are the one who can comfort yourself and give yourself the love and understanding that you needed but didn't get at the time.

☺

You can do this with any experience you want. It doesn't have to be a sexual related experience. It could be an experience where you remember being beaten by your mother or father. It could be one of being humiliated by a sibling. Any experience that comes to your mind that you remember wasn't a very pleasant experience, one that you bring up now and again, just in conversation with a partner or friend.

After doing this exercise you might find yourself crying from deep, deep within. You may feel your whole body, stomach and insides cry out. You may feel as though you want to push out of your body as though you are going to burst. Or you could even laugh uncontrollably. Whatever emotions you have, let them pour out. I know one woman who couldn't stop sneezing for over and hour.

The wonderful thing about doing these exercises is that afterward you feel lighter. It's just like when you hold onto tears, when you don't want to cry in front of someone, it actually feels like a pressure build up beginning in your stomach through to your chest, throat and moving into your head but when you let the tears flow you feel so relieved and refreshed.

You will come to the understanding that to be truly happy you will have to let go. When the time is right for you these feelings will begin to surface so that you can let them go and begin to live. The good thing is that these feelings only surface when you are ready to cope with them. You have nothing to be afraid of because you will not have to deal with more than you can deal with, you are not designed that way. That is the wonderful thing about you.

On the other hand you might feel nothing. When you find that you feel no emotions to an incident that left a mark on you as a child or adult then this is probably the incident that is holding you back the most. You may think it is irrelevant but it is probably the one incident that hurt you very deeply. This is a forgiveness emotion and I will explain more about this later.

There are different ways of releasing emotions even at night while you are sleeping you can be releasing negative emotions, through dreaming. You might notice you have a dream where you are screaming at someone, yelling at them as you never have or would in person. Or you might dream of crying so much until you are all cried out. These are all signs of progress. Everone is different and we all have different ways of releasing our emotions. You might want to exercise or dance out your feelings. You might want to listen to some music and sing as loud as you can. The secret is to let your feelings out don't bury them.

The question of sexual abuse may come up as you are going through the past. If you wonder whether or not you have been abused, well just asking the question means there are unresolved feelings that have to be explored. Nothing may have happened to you, but if in fact you have been wondering then this is another undealt with emotion.

Some children have been abused whilst sleeping or semi conscious and so you may never know for sure. I am not suggesting that every woman who has suffered with cystitis has been sexually abused but I do feel that they have some uncomfortable feelings with their sexuality. Be it through the taboo of talking about sex when they were growing up, or negative belief patterns held from generation to generation of how a girl *SHOULD* be decent, clean, proper, not showing any interest in sex, dressing appropriately and so on. Religion has also played a role in the guilt that many women feel over their sexuality.

After coming to the realization that bottled up emotions still holds the power to upset you, understand how they can create illness and can hold you back from living your life more fully.

☺

The past is over I choose to live in the now and learn from the past.

I let go of the need to please others.

I let go of the need to fear others.

I let go of the need to hold on to anyone.

I release it all and let go.

I am thankful for the process.

Working through past experiences helps you to understand yourself more clearly, perhaps identifying where certain fears or dependencies came from, or even how you may have formed an addiction, trying to bury your feelings. You might realize you were intimidated or humiliated by someone, and didn't understand the affect it still has on you. It could have been from a parent or sibling, uncle or even a teacher. This person may have hurt you deeply because you felt they were supposed to be there for you but let you down.

Write them a letter telling them exactly how you feel and how they let you down. Pour your heart out in this letter and at the end you could write "I let go of the need to expect you to be different from who you are" or "I forgive you for not being the (i.e. Dad) I needed". Then you can burn it and say farewell to that part of your life and move on. If you choose to send it to them think about your intentions for doing so. Is it to point the finger and blame them for *your* feelings or is it to heal your relationship?

When you release negative emotions towards others, at first you may feel frightened or angry but after these emotions have been released you can be free of the past and begin the relationship in the moment of now. You can decide if you want to continue the relationship or move on. You may find that you are now able to love people for who they are and not for whom *you* expect them to be.

If you decide to confront the person that you feel hurt you, you must remember that they have emotions too, when confronted they may not react the way you want them to. Don't be surprised if they aren't sorry or if they act defensive.

Often when confronting someone about the past they aren't ready for it and they may feel that you are attacking them. You have to understand that everyone is at different stages in life and that just because you are going through changes in your life, others may not be at that stage yet. In time, and it may take years, but in time and through your own healing you will notice a positive change in your relationship with the person who you feel has hurt you. Or you might decide that you don't really need them in your life anymore.

Questioning

Now its time to look at yourself and take some responsibility for what's going on in your life. It's good to look at our past and see where our feelings came from but now its time to look at why you hold on to them.

This section is a hard one because it no longer allows you to point the finger. It no longer allows you the comfort of blaming others for your problem. Do you have the courage to look at yourself in clarity? Let us see. Here are some questions to ask your self. Questions are a wonderful, wonderful gift. Questions promote growth.

****

What do you gain from your illness? Do you gain your partners guilt? Do you get out of things, like work, sex, or responsibilities? How do you make others feel when you are sick? Do they feel sorry for you? Does it make your partner lay off for a while?

If these questions make you angry or uncomfortable is it because they are touching the deeper truth about you?

It is time to let go and begin to trust in life. Only you have the ability to look at yourself and connect the thread, the tapestry of your own manipulative ways. We all learn to how to manipulate or control but why we do this is what we must gain an insight into. Are you willing to give up this form of control and move on to a new way of gaining what you desire?

Manipulation is what many people use in order to control others. The trouble with control is that it is not our true nature. God does not seek to control and never has, you see love is letting go and setting free. We must learn how to let go and begin to trust. We have been given free choice, learning to trust in free choice is our aim.

We tend to have a picture in our mind of how things should be and when they don't go according to our plan we find that we can't cope. This isn't how I wanted it to go, or this isn't how I planned (what ever it is) in my mind.

Do you feel that you have to control situations, or the people around you? Are you afraid that others can't or won't make the right choices for themselves? Do you believe others should think like you? Then it is time to let go and begin to trust in life.

This is where I feel we need to move into the discussion of religious beliefs and spirituality, of superstition and of trusting. You may be wondering what do my religious or spiritual beliefs have to do with me getting cystitis?

Learning to let go requires trust and if you find yourself not able to trust then perhaps your spirituality needs to be questioned.

I believe that we have deeply entrenched beliefs buried within us that have been passed on from generation to generation through religion and family that now have to be addressed. We are at a turning point in

☺

history and people are beginning to see that we need change. Our bodies are designed in the most powerful way to teach us that change is needed.

Questioning as I have said is the path to growth.

In the following pages I have put in many questions that I feel need to be asked. They are questions that you might find uncomfortable but I believe they must be asked if you want to grow as a person. Take time to think about them, ponder them and write down any feelings or thoughts that come to you.

Please try to write down as much as you can about each question so that you can look back and understand yourself more clearly............

Do you believe that we are all born in sin?

Is this a belief that you want to pass onto the next generation?

Is what you believe the only truth there is?

☺

Can you believe that what is true for you today may not be true for you tomorrow?

Do you believe that God will punish sinners?

How do you feel when you are having sex with your partner?

Do you have any guilt feelings after sex (feeling that you have done something wrong)?

Do you resent your partner or feel that he holds power over you?

Do you blame your partner for you not living up to the standard of your family or of God?

How do you feel when your partner wants to try different kinds of sex?

Do you think your partner or yourself are dirty or perverted?

Do you feel pressured by your partner?

How do you think you will be judged by God?

Do you pray for Gods forgiveness with regard to sexual activity?

Can you accept that truth is not static just as time is not static?

Is what you believe appropriate for this day and age?

Can you believe that God inspires people today?

Do you believe that the only way to know God is to study the Bible or Koran?

Can you accept that truth can expand with consciousness?

Do you believe that all things can be interpreted differently?

Can you believe that scripture can be interpreted by different levels of conscious awareness?

Are you involved in a religion because you feel obligated through family pressure?

Does your religion preach unity and love or separateness?

Does your religion make you feel that you are never quite good enough?

Are you afraid of what others will think of you if you change your beliefs?

Do you think you will be punished by God if you change your religion?

Do you believe that God loves all humans even those in other religions or atheists?

Who is acceptable?

☺

Do you believe that God only listens to the prayers of those in the right religion?

Is God love?

What is love in your opinion?

Do you trust in the power of love?

After doing this exercise can you see any thoughts or opinions that are holding you into a pattern of illness? Beliefs can change superstitions can be overcome. Learning to trust is the goal of all who are on the spiritual path. Trust is being able to let go and see the results without trying to control the outcome. You will find that when you let go of the reins the outcome is better than you could have imagined.

Every irritation is a form of growth. Our bodies use irritation as a way of getting our attention, when our body doesn't function in complete unity it lets us know that we aren't on the right track. To get on track we have to be willing to accept that perhaps we don't have all the answers and that maybe our beliefs have to be looked at and challenged.

When we look at nature we see life never stands still. The tides of the oceans keep moving, seeds keep sprouting new vegetation, and the earth keeps revolving. God has shown him / her self to be ever moving and not static. When a river or stream doesn't flow it becomes stagnant and polluted. Are you in the river of life flowing freely without fear? Or have you become stagnant? To become free flowing and not stagnant, involves many things, taking one step at a time opens the path to change.

We must be willing to let go of all that is no longer needed in our lives. If something is weighing you down then you need to off load it. The one truth we cannot deny is love. When we feel love we know we are on the right path.

Transforming The Old Into The New

Imagine being accepted and loved for who you truly are, exactly the way you are right now. If you want to be healthy, happy and feel free, you need to free your self of the burden of other people's opinions and ideas. Too many women and young girls feel the need to fit in and by trying to fit in and conform they become dead to their own beauty and their own uniqueness.

You need to take charge of your own life by repeatedly saying to yourself that you are perfect just the way you are, you are wonderful just the way you are. Start doing this and wait and see how wonderful life can be and how wonderful you will feel.

You can transform your whole life when you begin to trust, let go and allow love to flow through your life, this begins with loving thoughts and speech. Allow health to pour into you by pouring in healthy thoughts and words.

☺

Write one page of healthy spiritual thoughts and one page of how you feel along with any fears you might have. Reflect on these thoughts and take notice of any pattern in your thinking that needs to be challenged.

Here is an example of positive thoughts that will help transform your spirituality. When talking to yourself you can say I am or you are and end with your name. For example (I am valuable) or (you are valuable Diana).

I learn to interpret with love as my guide.

I let go of judgment, guilt and blame.

I am loving and love surrounds me.

I am joyful and joyfulness surrounds me.

I am peaceful and peace surrounds me.

I am kind and kindness surrounds me.

I am caring and others care for me.

☺

I am faithful and faith surrounds me.

I am forgiving and I am forgiven.

I have asked for Gods spirit and it has been given to me.

I have self control.

I am happy and happiness surrounds me.

I am healthy and health radiates from me and surrounds me.

I am full of love.

Beauty is everywhere and is also in me.

I allow life to flow through me easily.

My thoughts flow easily and happily.

I accept change with ease.

☺

I am positive and I accept myself.

I am safe.

My mind is fresh and open.

I am joyous and prosperous and I have loving people in my life.

I allow loving energy to flow through me.

Life is ever changing and I accept change with ease.

I am completely at ease with myself.

I am valuable.

I am worthy as is all creation.

I am thankful.

I am who I am

Pour out your heart in your thoughts and prayers. Ask for guidance and direction and it will be given. Keep questioning and pouring out your heart in prayer and write your feelings down in letters to God or to yourself.

I went through this myself and after weeks of confusion and turmoil I remember waking up one night, I don't know if I had a dream or what had happened, but I knew without any doubt that everything was going to be alright. I felt a complete calmness over me. I felt peace. No words can explain the gift that was given to me that night. That night I was given all the answers to every question in the universe. I awoke with the feeling of knowing, yet not being able to explain in human language these answers.

It was through deep prayer and meditation that my spirituality unfolded. I became more dependent on my personal relationship with God, through meditation and writing I found it easy to leave behind my dependency on religion and other people's approval.

☺

Through deep prayer and outpouring of my heart I found the answers to which I was searching. I found God to be revealing things to me that had never been revealed to me before and this gave me the strength I needed.

No one can come between you and your personal relationship with God. You don't need a middle man. You don't need someone telling you how to worship or how to please God. No one can come between you and Gods love.

I am convinced that neither death, nor life, nor angels, nor governments, nor things now here, nor things to come, nor powers, nor height, nor depth, nor any other creation will be able to separate us from Gods love.

Romans 8:38-39

Guidance is a lovely part of life, it's a gift that we all need from time to time. But remember we must be guided with love, when you are guided with guilt or fear then that is not love but manipulation of your emotions which is a form of control.

There is a scripture in the bible at Galatians Chapter 5:22 it reads:

..... the fruitage of the spirit is love, joy, peace, long-suffering, kindness, goodness, faith, mildness, self control. Against such things there is no law.

Notice the last fruitage is self control. What does this mean? How would you interpret this? If you interpret in a fearful way, you could imagine that it is saying you must control yourself because you might go wild, you might really sink to becoming a low person if you don't listen to your church, or society, or to anyone else who is telling you what is right and what is wrong.

How do you interpret?

I believe it is saying, when you learn to love yourself enough and are full of the fruitage of the spirit you no longer need to be controlled by others. When you have love and joy in your life, when you are long suffering and kind, when you are a good person and you have faith and you are mild, why would you need to be controlled by anyone except yourself?

And so there you have it **love does not seek to control**. God is love. **God does not seek to control**.

There is your freedom.

Guilt is devastating to the body

You see when you are guilty you must be punished and so therefore unconsciously you begin punishing yourself. Religion especially, works through making people feel not good enough or making people feel guilty, that is how they control, and that is how they gain power. It is not only religion that uses this form of control it is anyone who tries to make you feel guilty, friends, family society etc. Remember when someone tries to make you feel guilty or bad they are really trying to control or manipulate you.

When we learn to let go of trying to be right or trying to be perfect we can begin to live in freedom. To find peace of mind is to accept the all of everything and not to judge what is right and what is wrong and not to let others tell us what is right and what is wrong. Begin to understand that what is right for you may not be right for another and what is right for you today may not be right for you tomorrow. Things change, life is changing at each moment, it has to or everything would become boring stagnate and polluted.

If you believe you have found the one true religion the one true path to God, I would encourage you to think again. Love encompasses all and God is love. Who did Jesus say was the good Samaritan? Not someone of his own religion. Trust in God enough to look outside your safety zone. You will see love is in places you never allowed yourself to see before.

Love is in the bus load of disabled children who pass you by, waving all the way up the hill until you can no longer see them. Love is in a singing bird outside your window. Love is in places you least expect, just learn to be open to it.

In the bible there is a scripture at Matthew Chapter 7 verse 13-14 it reads:

"Go in through the narrow gate, because broad and spacious is the road leading off into destruction, and many are the ones going in through it, whereas narrow is the gate and cramped the road leading off into life, and few are the ones finding it.

Being guided by fear and guilt many people allow this scripture to keep them stuck in their religion believing that they are on the right path. That only those involved in their religion are of any value to God and everyone else is not quite as good as they are because they are not practicing their belief system. This goes for any religion quoting scripture to control the followers.

This scripture along with other scriptures can be interpreted another way.

"Go in through the narrow gate (which is love *unconditional*), because broad and spacious is the road leading off into destruction (fear and guilt lead to destruction) and many are the ones going through it, whereas narrow is the gate leading off into life (love breaths life back into you) and few are the ones finding it.

Interpret as you wish. How do you interpret?

Love is not just to be given to those who *you* choose to give it to. To those who think like you, that isn't true love. Love embraces all, *all.* Love is the breath of life.

Dark-Heavy Emotions	Light-Lighter Emotions
Fear	Love
Guilt	Self approval
Sadness	Joy
Anger	Acceptance
Blame	Forgiveness
Manipulation-control	Letting go and trusting
Competition	Unity
Jealousy	Inspiration
Closed in mind	Open to new ideas

Dark and heavy emotions weigh down the spirit and light emotions lighten your spirit.

When you fear – be it Satan or God or Man you cannot live life fully.

To fear Satan is to fear your own thoughts because Satan is an illusion of the mind something that mankind has created. Satan is fear and guilt. Fear and guilt

☺

produce sin. Fear and guilt cause the darkness and heaviness that we see on this earth.

If God is love then what have we to fear? Understand Love and you understand God. I could write pages and pages about God and Love but this is something that you have to find out for yourself. What I will say is that God is all. God is Complete. God is not separate from man, it is man that separates.

To fear Man is to fear yourself because man is a mirror of yourself, made in your image, your teacher and your friend.

When you let go of deep seated fears, deep insights will be given to you. You will be given more wisdom and more understanding as your reward. When you believe you are worthy of inspiration you will receive it.

As you move forward in your life and let go of your fears you will find inspiration and come to know that you are worthy of being inspired. You have your own connection to spiritual love.

Love is the key to spirituality. When you release negativity such as fear, guilt, anger, blame, competition, jealousy and wanting to control or tell others how to live their life, then you can allow the positive effects of love to flow through you.

You will come to know that there is spiritual help when you believe you are worthy of that help, when you believe that God is working for you and not against you. That you don't have to be afraid of God and you don't have to live up to some standard that only humans can define. The standard is love nothing more.

☺

Meditation

Meditation is a wonderful tool in healing I recommend you begin meditation as part of your healing process. Many people are afraid to meditate for various reasons but you must overcome this fear. People like to control everything and because meditation requires them to give up control of their thoughts they become afraid. This is a pattern of fear that needs to be challenged.

You will come to understand that letting go requires trust. To allow trust in your life is to give up control completely. When you give up control of your mind then you are truly trusting in intelligence far greater than your own. It is the connection of spirit.

If you are afraid to meditate then ask that the spirit of love surround you. Ask your God to watch over you and that healing energy will permeate you. If you have a question, ask it before the mediation and then let it go, don't try and think of an answer to your question while meditating. You must allow yourself to be free of all thought, to let go, relax and breathe.

    Find a quiet place to meditate that is clean and that you feel comfortable in. You can burn some incense if you like or light a candle. Sit on the floor with legs crossed and spine upright or in a comfortable chair. Have your hands relaxed by your side with palms facing up. Close your eyes and begin to relax your body, take notice of your abdominal muscles and begin to relax them, consciously work through your body and begin relaxing your chest, shoulders, arms, neck, jaw, tongue, unclench your teeth, relax the forehead. Have your chin parallel to the floor, so that the back of the neck is straight and the spine is lengthened, with your eyes closed focus between the eyebrows. Begin to take notice of your breath, the air going in through the nostrils will be slightly cool and the air that you breathe out will be slightly warm. Keep focusing on this, the air going in and out of the nostrils. Breathe quietly, relax and let go of any thought that comes into your mind. If a thought comes to you just say to yourself "let go, let go, I will think about that latter"

☺

then re centre your self and begin to focus once again on the breath.

While you are relaxed and meditating you may find that nothing dramatic has happened. What you will find is that your thoughts become clearer during the day and that you will find it easier to make decisions. The answer to your question will come to you either straight away or within the next day or so. Writing directly after meditating may also be helpful with any questions you have asked. Try to give yourself time to meditate everyday even if it's for 5-10 minutes. You will find your mind becomes less cluttered and less confused.

In life we are very busy with family, work, friends, television, recreation etc and it can be hard to find the time for meditation but this small amount of time can make a world of difference to your life. It can and will change your life for the better, giving you clarity and sharpness of mind. To become disciplined is the key.

I have found that a good meditation is to imagine that you are breathing in colours. The colour orange is associated with the bladder and sexuality. It is associated with the energy centre I talked about previously. The mental and emotional issues associated with this energy centre are guilt, blame, money, sex, power, control, creativity, ethics and honour. The physical dysfunctions associated with this energy are chronic lower back pain, sciatica, pelvic problems, sexuality and urinary problems. The organs affected by this energy centre are our sexual organs, large intestine, lower vertebrae, pelvis, appendix, bladder and hip area.

Imagine the colour orange as a large and fluffy cloud surrounding the area of the bladder, ovaries and vagina. Now imagine breathing it in and it filling up these areas. You can do this meditation while doing a yoga exercise which specifically deals with this area. Sit with the spine drawn up straight. Breathing in stretch tall, breathing out lean forward keeping the back, neck and head in a straight line, not bending the back or slouching. Move as far forward as is comfortable bringing the hands further down the legs now relax your neck, shoulders and arms, breathe in the colour orange for as long as you feel comfortable. Then when you come out of this posture lie on your back and relax for a few minutes.

You may like to find out more about colours and their healing properties. One interesting point to know is that white is the combination of all colours and black is the absence of colour. God is associated with white, (being complete) riding on the white horse etc. Satan is associated with black (being incomplete) riding the black horse. Like in the old movies the character that is good is dressed in white and the villain is dressed in black. If you delve into this subject more deeply you will no doubt become enlightened.☺

You may also like to find out more about the energy centres I have talked about. They are called chakras the chakras are the areas of interconnection between body and spirit. There are seven main chakras and each one correlates to specific organs in the body and emotions. It is said that through the practice of yoga these centres can become purified. There is a similar system which uses different terminology that is known in Taoism. I am not going to go into great detail here about them because my intention in writing this book is to help you heal cystitis not to direct you to follow any particular path. It is up to you to follow what interests you.

A Perfectly Balanced Mirror

I awoke from a beautiful dream which I believe was trying to telling me something I needed to know. I dreamt of a perfectly balanced mirror. It was oval in shape but I could see no reflection, there were three hooks on it which were the balancing factor.

My interpretation of this dream is as follows. The mirror represents God, being made in Gods image we are a reflection of God. There was no reflection because God is all and any one reflection would be less than God. The mirror was perfectly balanced as we must strive to be. The three hooks represented the mind, spirit and body, in whatever order you place them.

Where you need to find balance is up to you to decide. No on can tell you what it is you are holding onto or neglecting. You hold the key to your own healing, within you. I cannot hold out my key and say here is the key to your illness. What I can do is guide you. Interpretation of your illness is for you to individually interpret. You must empty the bucket of self destruction within you and move forward with love and joy. Whatever self destructive habits you have formed is for you to break out of. Whether it is a dependency on alcohol, cigarettes, prescription drugs, shopping, lying, stealing, deceiving others, whatever it is, you are the one who has to come clean with yourself. Even trying to look good can be a form of control. Many women try to manipulate men through their appearance. This will only drain you because it is another form of trying to control. There is nothing wrong with looking and feeling your best but understand your motives.

I had this dream because I needed to become balanced. If you are constantly suffering with cystitis then somewhere in your life there is an imbalance. You need to find balance and harmony in your mind, in your spirit and in your body.

We have talked about the mind and we have talked about the spirit and now we are going to talk about the body.

When I was suffering with cystitis I said to a friend of mine who has since passed away, if I ever find a cure for my suffering I will write a book about it. I have now been free of cystitis for well over 20 years. I wrote this book many years ago but couldn't finish it because I needed to be totally honest. I felt that I could write about the mind and the spirit but couldn't comfortably write about the body. I couldn't write about healthy eating because I wasn't following any kind of eating plan. I now feel the reason for this is because the food we eat has nothing to do with healing. This is the dilemma I found in finishing this book. Of course now I am drawn to eat lighter and healthier food, but this wasn't a factor in my healing, it came about naturally after many years of being free of cystitis.

The only constant thing I have done for my physical body is yoga and walking. I was drawn to yoga through an acquaintance who suggested I do yoga to help me with my cystitis. I loved it so much that I decided to study it for myself and subsequently became a yoga instructor. It was something that I was drawn to. You need to feel drawn to what feels right for you.

I had planned to give healthy eating advice and talk about healthy foods but the fact is that I have only had cystitis perhaps 2 or 3 times in 20 years whereas previously I had a cystitis attack every 2-3 months for 20 years. I have eaten all kinds of foods, so called healthy and unhealthy. I have gone on diets and restricted myself of foods that I like and then gone back to eating them again.

We have been bombarded with talk about healthy diets and healthy eating plans, but I have come to the conclusion that healthy eating can not be forced, it must come naturally. What we believe is good for our health today, may well be bad for us tomorrow. What we are told in the media about health can be changed in tomorrow's media. It's all about advertising, marketing and money.

I know of people who have never smoked or drank alcohol and have died of lung cancer or liver cancer. I know of people who have lived a long life well into their 80's or even 90's who have smoked a pack of cigarettes a day. In fact I recently meet a lovely Italian lady who invited me and my daughter into her house for a cup of

☺

Italian coffee. We had struck up a conversation with her as we passed by her house and she was kind enough to invite us in. I noticed that she smoked and she told us that she had smoked since she couldn't remember, she was 79 years old and still walked from her house to the shops with her trolley to get her groceries and loved where she lived.

I know of yoga instructors who are not vegetarians, who smoke and drink. I know of people who have been out jogging and have died of a heart attack.

The point I am trying to make is that we need not look outside ourselves for health. Guidance is good but never look at someone else as superior or take their word as gospel regarding what is good for you. All people will fall short of your expectations if you put them on a pedestal. Another one of my wonderful mothers sayings is "a professor isn't a professor in everything". No one person has the answer to everything. They can only guide you by what they know at the time. Yet time always changes.

I feel that guilt once again can be dangerous. If you feel guilty about what you do then this causes illness. If you eat something and feel guilty about eating it or are *made* to feel guilty then this is bad. I am not saying to have no conscience. I am suggesting that you take control of your choices and don't allow others to tell you what is good or bad for you.

    People may not like what I am saying here because there is a lot of money to be made in controlling people in all sorts of ways and also through a perception of health through diet. How many diet books are out there? How many companies make a lot of money out of diet supplements? How many magazines are sold marketing women and health?

    If you want to be healthy then you need to take charge of your own life. It is your own choices that create a healthy life for you. The key to health is to feel your way to it. When you decide to put something into your body take notice of your feelings *before* you eat or drink, take notice of how you feel *while* you are eating or drinking, and take notice of how you feel *after* you have finished eating or drinking or taking any other substance for that matter. If you feel good then that is good, if you feel any pain, bloating, heaviness, tiredness or irritation then that would be something to consider for next time.

Your body will tell you what is good for it and what is not. You don't need some corporation or government telling you what is good for you or bad for you. How many times have we been told that a certain food is good for us and then later down the track we are told that studies have found that the same food has been linked with cancer or some other disease.

The body does need to be nourished and treated well but the body needs to be fluid, there is no right or wrong in what you choose. It's being stagnant that is the problem and this happens to all people in different ways. Procrastinating, eating too much, drinking too much, smoking too much, watching too much television, shopping too much, gossiping too much etc, this is the problem. It is over indulging that is the problem. It helps to drain our energy. You need to take control of your life and begin to feel again, begin to have a passion and purpose again.

The most important aspect in being healthy is not to focus on diet but to focus on feeling good about you and feeling good within yourself.

It is balance that we need to aim for, a balance of joy and thankfulness in the rhythm of life. Being **thankful** for the food you eat and the water you drink is powerful. Many people say a prayer before a meal, saying thankyou to God for their meal. There are also many people that can't understand this concept because they think why should I be thankful when I am the one who has worked for it?

I believe if you **think** about the food you eat and drink and take the time to **ponder** how this food reached you then you would be very thankful for it. You don't necessarily have to thank God for it but you can be thankful for the food itself and for the process in how it reached you.

You will start to feel drawn to certain foods. I believe you will begin to know instinctively what foods your body needs. You may find yourself dreaming about certain foods, take notice of your dreams, perhaps they are trying to tell you to eat more of something that your body is lacking in, or to stop eating a particular food. I dreamt I was putting toxins all over my skin and that they were seeping into my body from the outside in, this made me decide to use soap with no chemicals or perfume. Dreams are there for your guidance.

Two of the kindest things you can provide your body with are oxygen and water. Your body doesn't need much to be healthy. Simplicity. Keep your life simple.

When you wake up in the morning breathe in the morning air and take notice of it, open your window or walk outside to breathe it in. Drink a glass of water then fill up a litre bottle of water and drink this during the day, also every time you urinate drink a glass of water. Remember when you release fluid you must fill up with fluid. Before you go to bed drink a glass of water this is very important, also if you get up at night to go to the toilet, drink a glass of water. This will become a good habit.

    I would like to bring to your attention now an important point, when you feel the urge to urinate, don't. Sound strange? You need to build up a strong and healthy bladder, when you feel the urge to go to the toilet just take notice and then continue doing whatever it is you were doing, you may notice that you no longer need to go. Your mind plays tricks on you and you must begin to control your mind and your body and in this case the bladder. So the aim is not to go to the toilet with the first urge or with the second but to go on the third urge. This way the bladder will be full and this helps to flush out the urinary tract, make sure you empty the bladder completely, don't rush in and rush out of the toilet, take your time to fully empty the bladder. Then drink a large glass of water when finished.

☺

Once again you could use writing to help you with cleansing your body. I have written some helpful lines which can open up your consciousness to health.

I am ready to listen to my body's needs

I am willing to understand my body's messages

I let go now of abusing my wonderful body

I am ready to move towards health

It is my intention to become fit, healthy and fully inspired.

I comfortably let go of anything that holds me back.

I am excited about the freedom I have to pursue my dreams.

I am ready now to let go of the past.

Many women who suffer with cystitis also suffer with constipation. Constipation is associated with holding on, being in a hurry, and not drinking enough water. When you free yourself emotionally and spiritually and eat the foods that are right for you along with exercise and enough water, you will also find that you no longer suffer with constipation. When sitting on the toilet you need to relax. Men seem to be able to do this easily but women tend to rush themselves.

Also often when we are not feeling well we think what can I take to feel better? What can I put into my body to make me feel better? When in most cases the absence of food or drink is better for us. For example if you have a stomach upset from eating food that doesn't agree with you, you might think if you eat something else or take some tablet you will feel better. But sometimes it is better to give your body time to eliminate the problem. Your body is designed to heal and cleanse itself, trust in it. We can use breathing techniques and exercise to eliminate toxins in the body.

I suggest you start some kind of exercise. Walking is an easy thing to do and it doesn't cost anything. Try getting up earlier in the morning and go for a walk, sometimes it's hard to make the move but once you start you will realise how good you feel afterwards. Move towards what attracts you, you may want to try Pilates, Yoga, Tennis, Line Dancing or Swimming just make some kind of start.

If you find yourself getting more attacks of cystitis don't give up. As our bodies begin to heal sometimes the symptoms appear worse. They can regress through the time line of the dis-ease. It may be that it is working its way out. As with any detox program you may feel worse to begin with but it is cleaning your system out. I went through this myself nearing the end of my journey, I started to have a surge of cystitis but this time instead of being afraid, I let go and I said to myself if this is what I have to go through in life then so be it. I thought of all the other people in life who go through suffering and hardships, people who are blind, people who are quadriplegics, people who have diabetes, and people who have been through other tragedies. I completely surrendered and accepted my fate. It was then that I felt a shift.

The truth is you need to love who you are with all your so called imperfections. Love the imperfections. Stop judging. Everyone will tell you, you shouldn't do this or you shouldn't do that, you have to eat this or you have to eat that. Stop listening to everyone else and begin to listen to your inner voice.

There seems to be too many rules in life. When you love and trust yourself you begin the journey of self discovery and self control. Enjoy the process, stop being so hard on your self. If you need to be weak for a moment in time then be gentle on yourself. Everyone has weaknesses, that is the beauty of life, to be able to love and support one another, to care for ourselves and to care for others. Life is for living and for experiencing, there are many loving people in this world who are caring and supportive, move towards them, become one of them.

A nice thing to do for yourself is to get some magazines (not the gossip celebrity ones) and cut out pictures of things that you like, for example places you would like to travel to or people that inspire you. The new car you have always wanted. Things that you are drawn to, like a hobby you have wanted to do or even cut out words that make you feel good and stick them on a sheet of coloured paper. Pin it up somewhere so that you can see it, seeing this will help your subconscious mind draw it to you. You are drawn to it and it will be drawn to you.

Visualise yourself being completely happy and healthy. When going to sleep at night instead of thinking about the past and wasting time worrying about the future or feeling guilty about things you have said or done, see yourself exactly the way you would like to be. See yourself clearly in a scenario that makes you feel happy. Picture yourself as though you are in a movie, see yourself doing what you love, see the people that you care about all living a fulfilled and happy life, feel as though it is true. How much nicer is it to fall asleep with wonderful thoughts than to fall asleep worrying?

If you had a bad day and feel that you wished things could have been different, as you go to sleep at night instead of playing the whole bad day back in your mind, change it to the way you would have liked it to be. Imagine that you could change the scene, just like a movie director. In your mind play the scene over but this time change it to how you would have wanted it to be.

This has powerful effects on the subconscious mind, as the subconscious mind takes notice of the imagination.

Some simple techniques to release toxins and unblock energy

There are a few simple breathing exercises I would like to share with you and some postures too. To me they are too important to leave out because I feel they can help not only people with cystitis but everyone.

An easy way to bring energy flow into your body is to do the following exercise.

Get yourself an exercise mat and set yourself up in a nice area of your house that feels good for you. Open your window to let in some fresh air.

Stand at the top of the mat and bring your feet together, big toes touching each other, or feet hip width apart, what ever feels more comfortable. Lift and spread the toes and replace them on the mat. Spread the weight evenly through the feet lifting the arches a little. Close your eyes and feel your balance, lengthen through the legs, lifting the knee caps and tucking the tail bone under, lengthen through the spine bring the shoulders back and down, allow the fingers to stretch down, lengthen through the neck with your chin parallel to the floor. Imagine some one pulling a cord through your spine and out through the top of your head pulling and lengthening you. Slowly as you breathe in, bring your arms out to the side and up over your head, filling the lungs. As you breathe out, bring the arms down slowly, emptying the lungs. Do this three times with full awareness then open your eyes.

The following exercise is called "Surya Namaskar" which translates to Salute to the Sun, it is a nice flowing exercise which incorporates breath.

Bring your hands together in prayer position and relax your shoulders, arms and elbows down. Breathe in, breathe out bring your arms down beside your legs, breathing in bring your arms forward and raise them up over your head and gently arch your back as far as you feel comfortable.

Breathe out, bend forward, bending the knees if necessary and bring your hands down to rest beside your feet.

Breathe in, step the right leg back.

Step the left leg back so that you are in a plank position. Hold the breath.

Breathe out and bring your knees, chest and chin to the mat.

Breathe in sliding forward, stretch up and raise the head with your back slightly arched.

Breathe out and lift the hips and bottom up and push through with the hands.

Breathe in and step the right foot forward toward the hands.

Breathe out and step the left foot forward allow the head to relax down toward the knees.

☺

Breathe in, bring the arms forward and rise them up over the head and gently arch your back as far as feels comfortable.

Breathe out and bring the arms back over the chest into prayer position relaxing the shoulders, arms and elbows.

Take a few breaths and begin the sequence again only this time you step back with the left leg.

After you have done this lie down on your back, tuck your chin in a little so the back of the neck is straight and allow the arms to relax beside your body with your palms facing up, if you like you can put a pillow under your knees. Relax for 5 or 10 minuets starting with relaxing your toes, feet, ankles and moving up through your whole body until you feel peaceful and relaxed.

****

We all know that we have to breathe or we would die but not many people think about it at all and many people only breathe in shallow breaths. Oxygen brings vital energy to our whole being.

We have two nostrils and usually one nostril is partially blocked. This normally alternates between nostrils throughout the day and each cycle lasts for around one and two hours. You may think big deal who cares? It doesn't really matter if there is a balance but when one is dominant then there could be problems.

When doing my yoga training we had to study the effects of breathing in through one nostril. For one week we had to sit quietly for 10 minutes a day and block off one nostril and breathe normally through the other and then write down any effects on our mood etc. The following week we had to do the same on the other side. I noticed that one week I felt a little more introverted and even a little teary, then the following week I felt much more aggressive and angry.

It was only later that I found out that if you breathe through the left nostril it is connected to the right brain hemisphere and its nature is thought to be feminine and peaceful. If you breathe through the right nostril it is connected to the left hemisphere and is associated with everything masculine and aggressive.

To bring balance to the breath there are some simple techniques.

A simple breathing exercise to do is to sit quietly with your spine straight use your right hand and block off your right nostril gently with your thumb and breathe through your left nostril for seven normal breaths without straining or forcing. Then use your right ring finger to gently block off your left nostril and breathe through your right nostril for seven breaths. Take notice of which nostril is more blocked than the other. It doesn't really matter just take notice.

Now continue to alternate your breathe by blocking the left nostril breathe in through the right, block off the right and breathe out through the left, breathe back in through the left and breathe out through the right, breathe in through the right, breathe out through the left, breathe in through the left, breathe out through the right. Continue this for about 5 minutes.

If you want to go further you can begin a count. Count in for 6 counts and out for 6 counts.

As you get used to this you can add a hold. Count in for 6 counts, hold the breath for 2 counts, breathe out for 6 counts, do not breathe in again for 2 counts. Then repeat.

When you feel comfortable with this, place your middle and index finger in between the eye brows and continue.

It's good to do this exercise for 5-10 minuets a day if you can. I like to do this just before mediation.

Please note that it is good to inhale through your nose as much as possible, breathing in through the mouth can cause dizziness, nervousness and other physical and emotions problems. Mouth breathing also accelerates water loss increasing possible dehydration.

☺

My Happy Face Tips

Always say loving things to yourself especially when you are feeling afraid. "Love surrounds me and permeates me".

You are worthy of intimacy and love. If it is your will to become healthy this must become part of your belief system.

Make it your aim to drink a large glass of water after going to the toilet. (If you release fluid you must replace it).

Don't race to the toilet with the first urge, try to hold on for a little longer until the bladder is full and make sure you empty it completely.

Drink a glass of water before and after sex and always pee after sex.

Use a non perfumed soap.

☺

Guilt is destructive, it destroys the life force. If you feel that you have done or are doing something wrong, either stop doing it or stop feeling guilty. Do no make your partner feel guilty either.

Make it your aim to let out your feelings by writing them down at least once a week.

Allow yourself time to meditate it will help you to have a clearer understanding of yourself.

Try not to allow yourself to become constipated. Your body will be building up toxins when constipated.
(use a good probiotic preferably with cranberry)

Make it your intention to become completely at ease with yourself.

Drink lots of water and you could try Cornsilk tea and Dandelion tea.

Burn essential oils specifically known to help with cystitis. I have listed some at the end of this book.

The Key To The Future

Forgiveness

The key to the future is forgiveness. Forgiveness of yourself and all your so called mistakes and forgiveness of others.

If your aim is to have a bright and fully inspired future you must let go of the past. The key to letting go of the past is forgiveness. If you have chosen not to fully forgive someone then you are still holding onto emotions which will block you and cause illness. Inspiration will flow when you are free of emotional ties.

Just saying ok I'm prepared to forgive is not enough. You have to want to truly forgive and to make it your intention to never bring up the matter again either discussing it with others or to bring up the matter in your heart. This is why it is very powerful. You have to be ready to do this.

If you have gone through the exercises in this book then you will have a clearer understanding of who it is you need to forgive. Sometimes the person we need to forgive may no longer be alive. It is still necessary to forgive them to move on yourself. I will give you a guide to a forgiveness ritual you can do to help you finally let go. Do not do this until you feel that you are ready.

There is no right or wrong way to do this but your intentions must be pure, you must be willing to forgive and forever let go of any hurt, bitterness, sadness or anger connected with this person. Before you begin make sure you will not be disturbed. Turn your phone off and do this some where you feel safe and comfortable. Make sure you are away from a smoke detector or disconnect it until you are finished.

As you are preparing you might like to listen to some of your favourite music and burn some essential oils.

You will need some pure water as a symbol of purity in your intention. You can use some bottled water that you have never tried before. There are many different varieties in the supermarkets. Or you can use some filtered water from your home it's up to you. You will also need a bowl to burn a letter of release in. It needs to be a fire proof bowl of course. Burning is a symbol of purification, the end of something which opens the way to new beginnings.

Write down your intentions and say a prayer confirming them. For example you could say "My intention today is to release and cleanse myself of all toxic emotions attached to eg: my father". You can then ask for help through prayer in doing this. Pour some water into a glass and drink it. Say to yourself "This is a symbol of me purifying my body of all toxic emotions my intention to forgive eg: my father is pure".

Now write a letter of release, begin to write all your hurt feelings towards the person that you are about to forgive. Tell them exactly how hurt you have been and how they made you feel. This will be the last time you ever express your feelings about this incident so get it all out every last bit of it. Go into detail tell them how they

☺

let you down and how they weren't the person you wanted them to be for you. Don't rush this process because remember it will never be brought up again. At the end of the letter you must write that you are now prepared to let it all go and that you are finally prepared to let them go and live their life in peace. Now read the letter out loud as though you are reading it to them. Sit with your feelings for as long as you need to.

It is now time to burn the letter and release forever the bond. You can say "This is a symbol of me burning fire outside of myself instead of burning within I now blow out the fire within me and I'm ready to begin again".

This ritual is very powerful it releases painful destructive energy and opens the floodgates to new clear energy.

After doing this myself I noticed I couldn't stop laughing. I laughed so much and for so long my stomach ached.

All the sadness was gone.

In Closing

Health is a continuing process, there is no quick fix. It is a process of looking within yourself every day. Learn to enjoy the process and not to dread it. Life is full of wonder and mystery, you yourself are mystical. We are all going through the journey of life together and we are never alone.

Remember you can read a book and be guided by it but don't allow it to become a bible to you, nothing is static.

Life is like a hauntingly beautiful song. When you hear that special song you may play it over and over, wanting to hear it for its beauty until you have heard it enough and then you move onto a new song.

Essential Oils

Bergamot: Is believed to help with

Physical: Sore throats, fevers, intestinal colic, slow digestion, respiratory infections, lost appetite, cystitis.

Mental: Helps anxiety, emotional imbalance, stress and nervous tension, balancing and calming.

Eucalyptus: Is believed to help with

Physical: Influenza, bronchitis, asthma, throat infection, laryngitis, fever, rheumatism, sports injuries to muscles, cystitis and bladder infections.

Menta: Stimulant to increase concentration, relieves nervous tension.

Juniper Berry: Is believed to help with

Physical: Rheumatism, gout, arthritis, digestive system, sore muscles, cystitis, cirrhosis, fluid retention.

Mental: Strengthens and uplifts low energy.

Sandalwood: Is believed to help with

Physical: Diarrhoea, cystitis, sinusitis, cramps.

Mental: Calms nervous tension, stabilizing and balancing, helps meditation.

Lavender: Is believed to help with

Physical: Headache, wounds, rheumatism, asthma, influenza, high blood pressure.

Mental: Reduces stress, calms anger, relaxes insomnia and tension Uplifting and balancing in depression.

Notes

www.ingramcontent.com/pod-product-compliance
Lightning Source LLC
Chambersburg PA
CBHW071517040426
42444CB00008B/1687